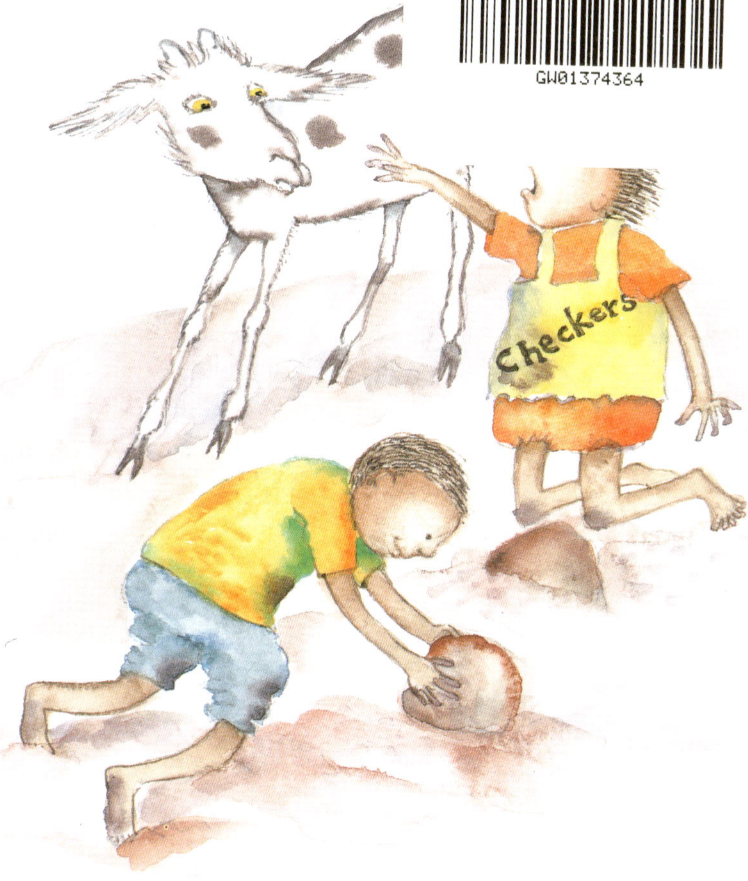

Let's make a house.

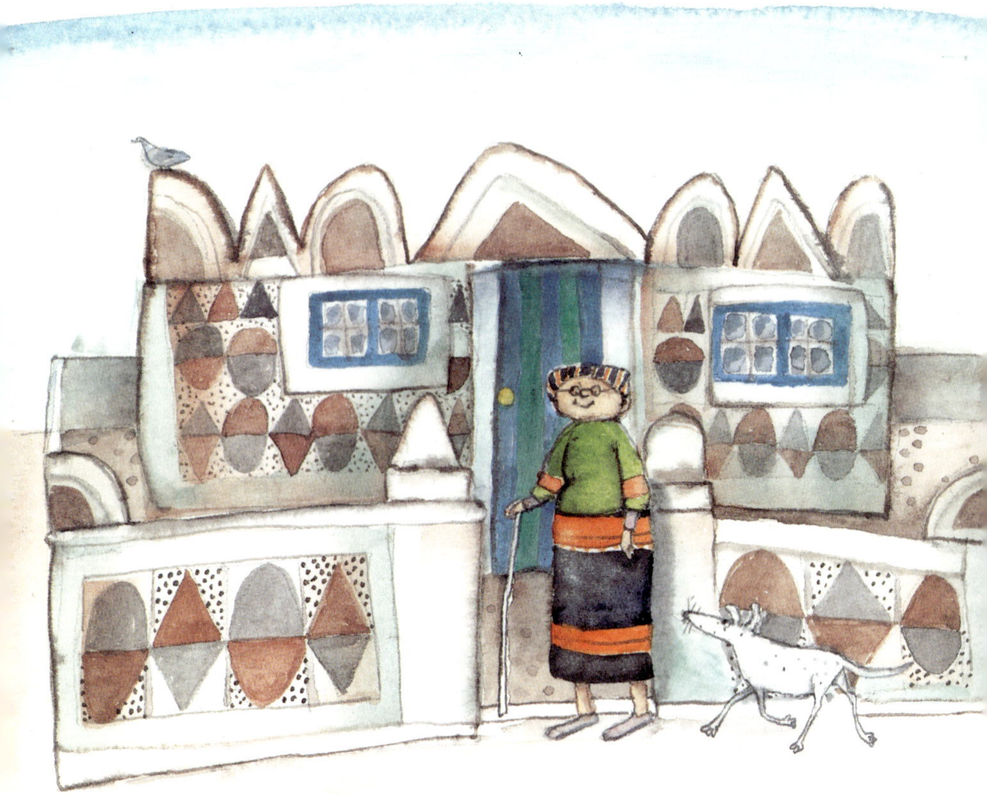

Will it look like this?

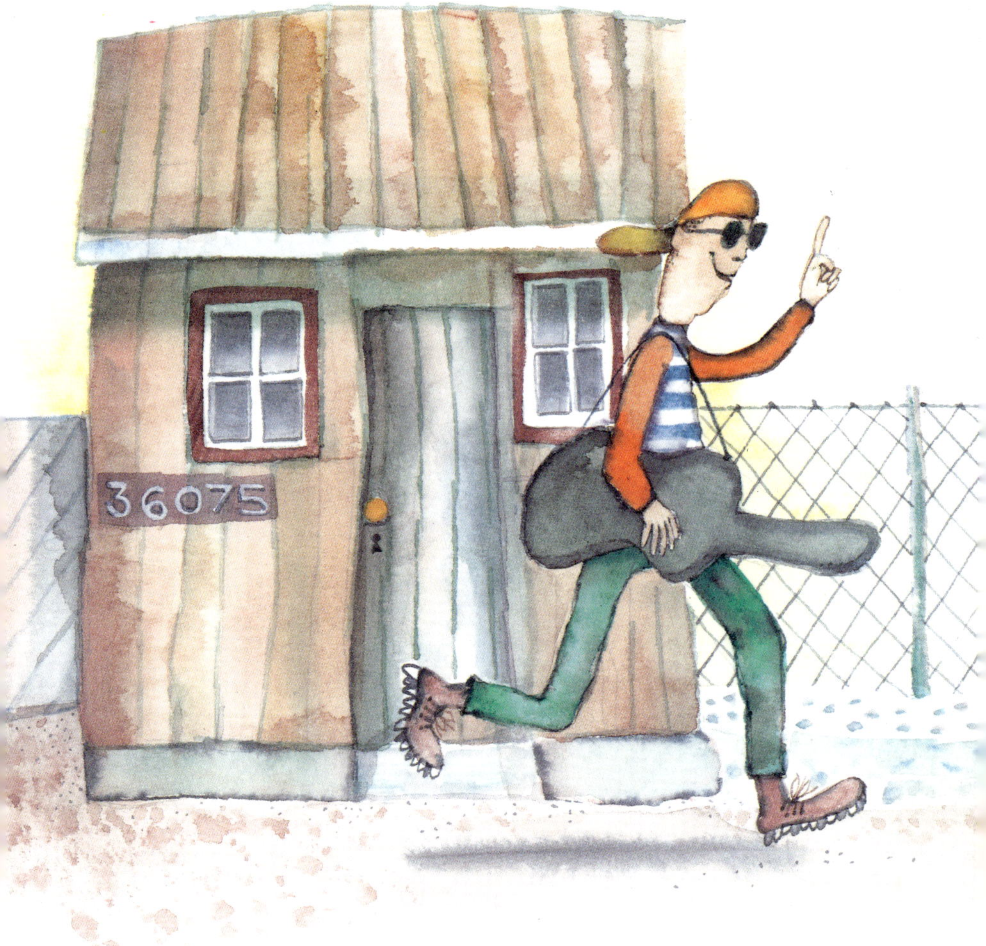

Will it look like this?

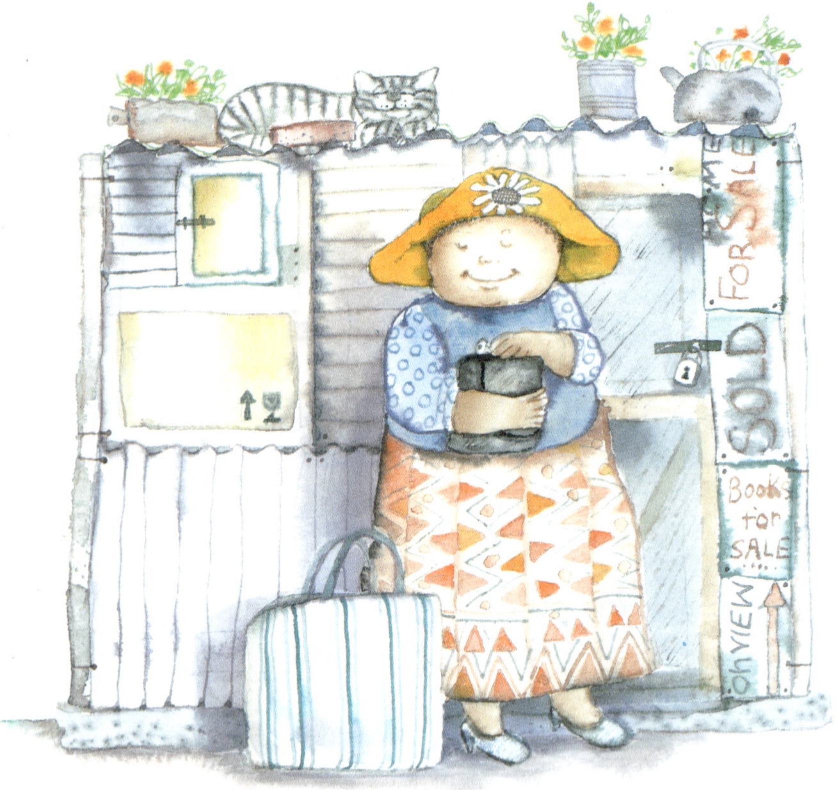

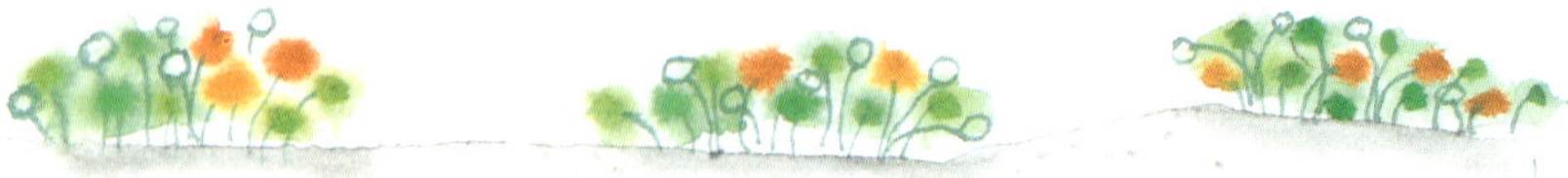

Or will it look like this?

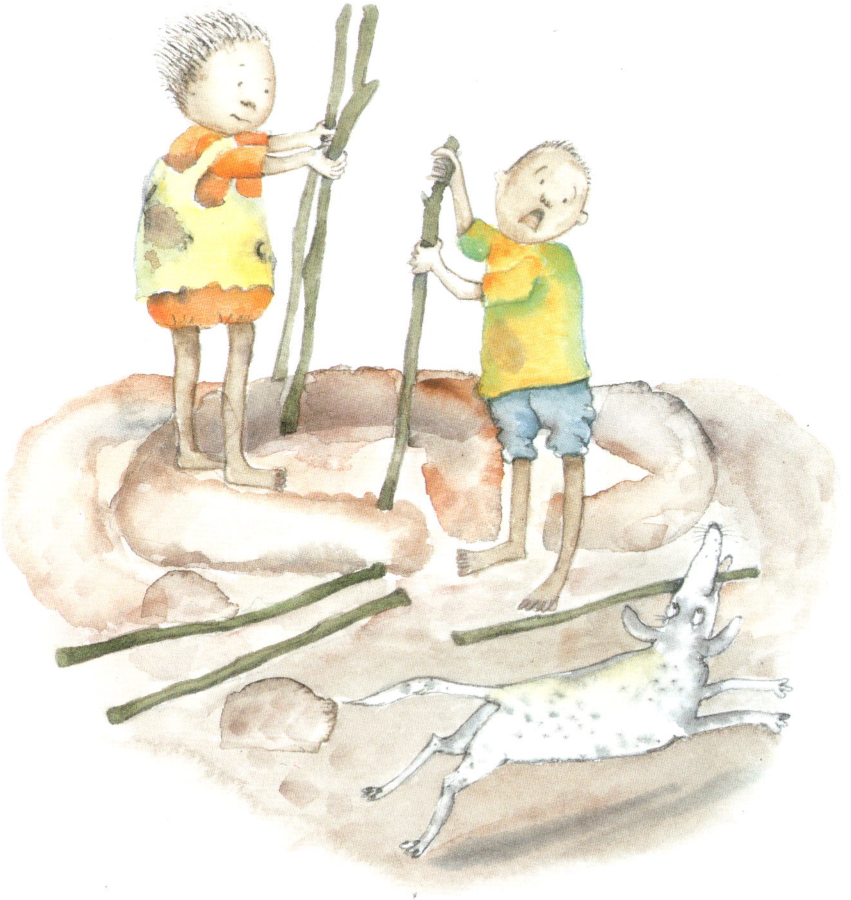

We can use mud and sticks.

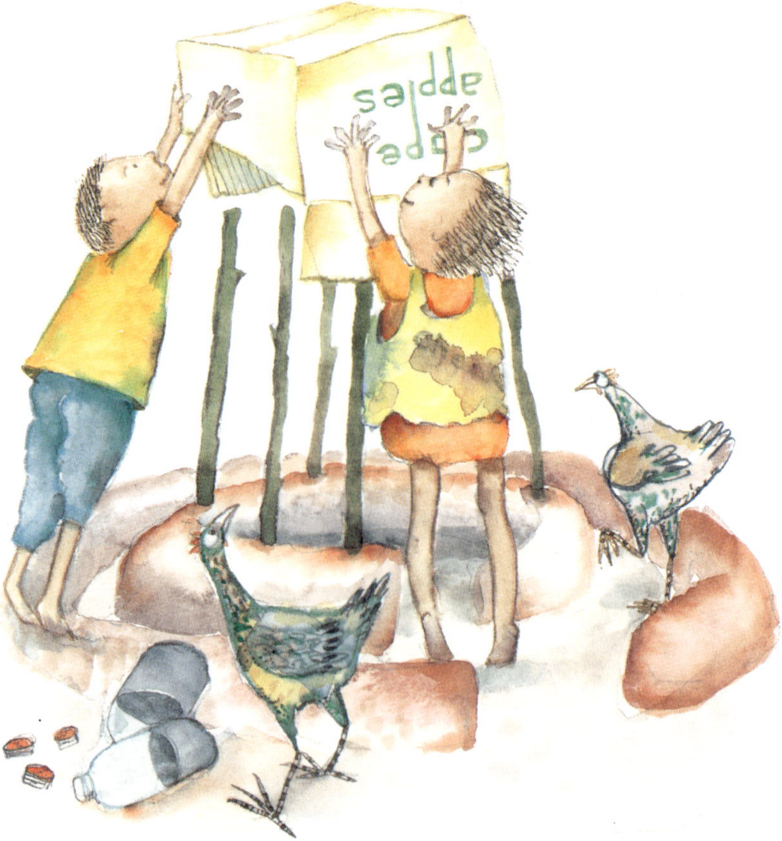

We can use this box.

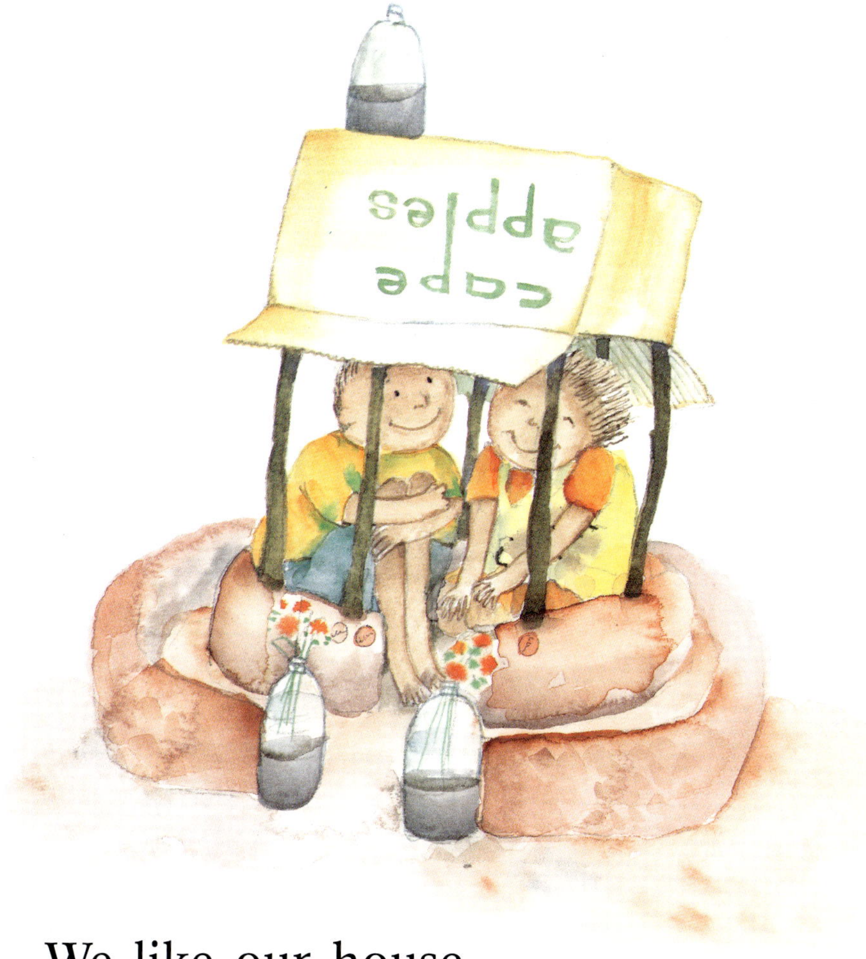

We like our house.

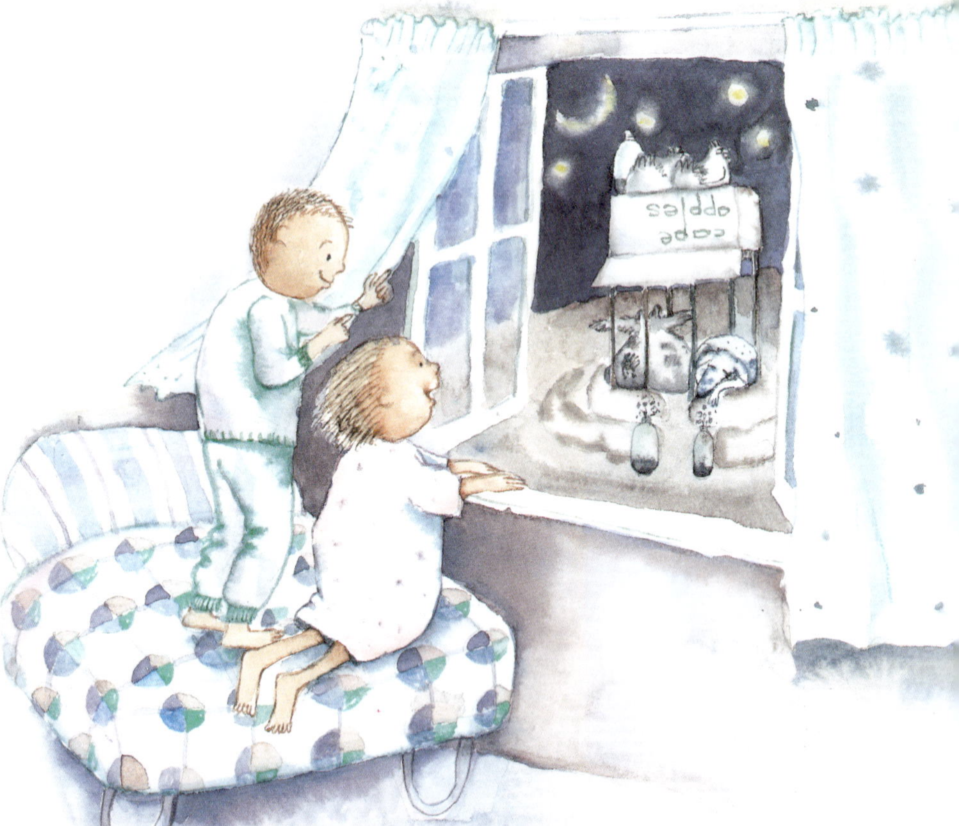
cape apples